SIMPLE

FURNITURE MAKING

How to Make Tables, Chairs, Bookshelves, Sideboards, Chests, Kitchen Accessories, etc.

With Twenty-Three Illustrations

BY

SIDNEY VANT

British Library Cataloguing-in-Publication Data
A catalogue record for this book is available from the
British Library

Making and Restoring Furniture

Furniture is the mass noun for the movable objects intended to support various human activities, such as seating, storing, working and sleeping. Most often, at least in the present day - furniture is the product of a lengthy design process and considered a form of decorative art. In addition to furniture's functional role, it can also serve a symbolic or religious purpose, for instance in churches, temples or shrines. It can be made from many materials, including metal, plastic, and wood, using a variety of techniques, joins and decoration, reflecting the local culture from which it originated. Furniture construction can be extremely technical, or very simple, dependent on the desired end product and skills of the maker.

Numerous courses are available to provide a grounding in furniture making, generally designed to broaden practical (as opposed to art historical) knowledge of materials, tools and design. For the amateur maker, such options can be an extremely useful route into building and restoring their own furniture. Typically, restoring furniture has been seen as a job solely for the trained craftsman, however with the advent of readily available courses, books and online tutorials, it has never been easier to start yourself. Furniture construction and restoration does take a good deal of preparation and persistence, not to mention a keen eye for detail, but can be successfully achieved by any enthusiastic individual.

One of the first things to assess, is what to look out for when purchasing (or evaluating your own) old furniture. As a general rule, if you are restoring furniture yourself, look for older mass-produced items, produced after the mid-nineteenth century. These (with some exceptions) will not have very high values, but are incredibly well made - able to last a long time in the family home. If in doubt, do ask an expert however! One should also be aware, that there are certain more recent styles and designers of furniture which are incredibly rare, for example Art Deco, Arts and Crafts, De Stijl and Bauhaus. Another key thing to look out for are 'dovetail joints'; they are strong and require skill to assemble, and are thereby generally a good sign of a well-constructed piece of furniture. Solid wood or plywood backing, for instance on the back or inside of drawers, are also good indicators of age, as solid wood will generally tell you that it is pre-twentieth century, whereas plywood was only utilised after this date. Perhaps more obviously, inscriptions and manufacturer's stamps can tell the owner a lot about their piece of furniture.

Painting and stencilling wood furniture is probably the most common, and easiest starting activity for the amateur furniture restorer. When finishing wood, it is imperative to first make sure that it has been adequately cleaned, removing any dust, shavings or residue. Subsequently, if there are any obvious damages or dents in the furniture, wood putty or filler should be used to fill the gaps. Imperfections or nail holes on the surface may be filled using wood putty (also called plastic wood;

a substance commonly used to fill nail holes in wood prior to finishing. It is often composed of wood dust combined with a binder that dries and a diluent (thinner), and sometimes, pigment). Filler is normally used for an all over smooth-textured finish, by filling pores in the wood grain. It is used particularly on open grained woods such as oak, mahogany and walnut where building up multiple layers of standard wood finish is ineffective or impractical.

After the furniture is thus smartened, it should then be sanded (without entirely removing the finish) and primed before a base coat of paint is applied. Aerosols will provide a smoother finish than paintbrushes. If stencilling afterwards, make sure that the base colour is completely dry before the final step is embarked upon.

Recovering dining room chairs is another popular activity, involving skills with fabric as well as woodwork - also fashionable is metal furniture restoration. Metal work provides slightly different problems to those of traditional wood and chair restoring; one of the main questions is - do you actually want to make the piece 'as good as new?' Rust and signs of wear can be removed to varying degrees, with many choosing to leave their pieces of furniture worn and torn; achieving 'the industrial look', popular in design circles. This is especially the case for small-scale furniture like lighting, various ornaments such as candlesticks and even larger pieces such as cast-iron beds. If a metal piece is going to be painted, it is imperative to first remove the rust however. This is a time consuming, but ultimately rewarding task to complete, and can be done by a professional for larger objects. Once the metal is rust free, all that remains is to prime and paint! Antiquing effects can also be used, i.e. sanding off layers of paint (of differing colours if the maker prefers) - finished off with a clear protective finish.

Today, British professional furniture makers have self organised into a strong and vibrant community, largely under the organisation 'The Worshipful Company of Furniture Makers', commonly referred to as the Furniture Makers or the Furniture Makers Company. Its motto is 'Straight and Strong'! Members of the Company come from many professions and disciplines, but the common link is that all members on joining must be engaged in or with the UK furnishing industry. Thus the work of the Company is delivered by members with wide ranging professional knowledge and skills in manufacturing, retailing, education, journalism; in fact any aspect of the industry. There are many similar organisations across the globe, as well as in the UK, all seeking to integrate and promote the valuable art that is furniture making. Education is a key factor in such endeavours, and maintaining strong links between professional practitioners, didactic colleges and the amateur maker/restorer is crucial. We hope the reader enjoys this book.

CONTENTS

SIMPLE FURNITURE MAKING

SECTION I

EQUIPMENT

UNTIL recently it was usual to regard the man who made his own furniture as mildly eccentric and, as a matter of fact, the rather odd designs evolved often went a long way towards justifying the opinion. Within the past few years, however, furniture making has become a popular hobby, and it is notable that ladies as well as men find it interesting and useful, and certainly economical.

The reasons for this change can be traced to the high price of furniture immediately after the War. Adventurous souls tried their hands at furniture making, their success emboldened others, and then the commercial houses lent a hand by supplying neat mouldings, panellings, turned legs, etc., not to mention machine-finished woods in popular dimensions. But most of all it is due to the greater simplicity of furniture design now ruling. Except for a light bead, or a modest medallion, much of the furniture sold to-day is devoid of all " frills." That it is not less pleasing than that of a generation ago is attributable to the fact that the design is better ; it can stand by itself without the meretricious aid of fearful and wonderful fretwork "ornamentation." All this, of course, has greatly smoothed the path of the amateur constructor, and the man or woman with a very modest amount of skill can with patience and a reasonable amount of care turn out presentable articles of furniture. Needless to say, one should begin with simple articles—the surest guide to success in these matters is knowledge of one's limitations.

In the pages that follow we describe the making of a series of articles of furniture, starting with the very simplest form of bookshelf and passing to jobs of greater difficulty. We also include hints on making one or two typical articles of kitchen furniture. We cannot describe every kind of furniture-making job the amateur is likely to tackle, but we shall endeavour to give as many as possible of the joints and methods in general use, so that the novice who proposes to buy components, such as legs, mouldings, etc., and from them make up a piece of furniture, should have no difficulty in deciding how to set about the job.

TOOLS

All the work outlined in the pages that follow can be done with the aid of such simple tools as lie in the average householder's toolbox. A medium-weight hammer, a gimlet and a screwdriver will be required. A wooden mallet can be added to the hammer by way of a luxury, but is not really essential. A smoothing plane is also required. These can be procured either with wood or metal stocks ; but it is better to have the plane, of whichever material, on the large size rather than too small. A good-sized smoothing plane will do all the work required, and it should not be necessary to include a long jack plane in the kit. Two saws will be needed : a hand saw for ripping boards and similar work and a tenon saw for cutting out joints, etc. The larger saw should not be too coarse-toothed, or it will tend to tear away the edges of the wood being cut. When not in use, saws should be kept in a dry place, and an occasional wipe with an oily rag will keep them free from rust and do much to prevent sticking when in use.

One or more chisels will be needed ; the sizes are indicated in the description of work on later pages. A half-inch chisel is a useful size, though it may be considered more useful to have a pair : one quarter-inch and one either three-quarters or one inch in width. Chisels and planes are delicate tools, strong as they appear, and great care should be taken of their cutting edges. After use the plane iron should always be withdrawn, to protect it from damage, and if chisels cannot be kept in a rack they should at least be stored in such a way that their fine edges are not likely to be thrown against hard objects, such as a hammerhead.

A glue-pot may be considered a luxury by those used to making shift with tins or jam-jars, but the cost of a proper pot is small, and they are more efficient. It is not necessary to get a large pot unless a great deal of glueing is to be done. Re-heated glue is always weaker than freshly-made glue : "little and often" is the motto for glue-makers.

It is a common ambition of all householders to own a proper bench, and no doubt one can do good work with such equipment. But the absence of a bench is no excuse for not tackling any of the jobs outlined here, nor is there any reason to anticipate that the work will be less satisfying because of its absence. The uses of a bench are, broadly, two-fold :

(*a*) To serve as a table on which to lay wood for planing, marking, etc. A stout kitchen table is just as effective for these purposes. For planing it is necessary to insert a stop-screw into the end of the table, in order that the end of the board may rest against it during planing. A screw should be used in preference to a nail because the height of the stop is then easily regulated by a few turns with a screw-driver to right or to left.

If it is not desired to put screws into the table, all that is necessary is a one-inch board not less than eight inches wide and four inches longer than the table. At either end of this board, and on the same side of it, fix two pieces of two-inch battening so that their outer edges are flush with the end of the board, and their inner edges, when the whole is laid over the table, will lie against the ends of the table. The board will thus be held firmly in position over the table, and a screw may be put into the board without any fear of injury to the table.

EQUIPMENT

Where the table available is not very strong it is wise to make such a board as that described above, cutting it at least a foot longer than the table and leaving one end projecting beyond the table in such a way that it can be brought against a wall. Then, when planing, the forward push is taken by the wall, and no undue strain is thrown upon the table legs. The forward end of the board should be suitably padded so that it does not injure the paint-work or the wall.

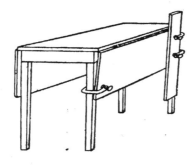

Fig. 1

(b) The other use of a bench is as a support for a vice in which wood can be conveniently held for working. There are several ways in which this advantage can be applied to the kitchen table. In the first place, small table vices can be bought for a few shillings, and these are quite satisfactory for small jobs—the vices are really made to hold metal jobs. Those using a table with a drop-flap (See Fig. 1) can utilise iron clamps such as are used to affix portable mangles, etc., to tables. Let the flap side of the table down, and with one clamp fix it to the leg so that it is quite rigid. All that is necessary now is to fix the piece of work against the flap side with the aid of other clamps.

Those who have no flap side to their table can generally utilise the drawer of a dresser, but the best way of using a drawer is to make a box of exactly the same size, so that it fits exactly into the aperture, and to use this box as a base for a proper wooden bench screw, to be bought at any iron-monger's or woodshop for about half-a-crown. If you do not want to make a separate box to replace the drawer, you may be able to arrange to attach the bench screw to the *back* of the drawer (the drawer being inserted back to front in such a case) ; but everything depends upon the drawer, and in any case the greater part of the screw would have to be detached after every job.

If much glueing is to be done, one other kind of clamp is necessary and can be readily improvised. All that is necessary is a one-inch board, four or five inches wide and about six inches longer than the largest piece of work likely to be clamped in it. Across each end of this board fix firmly two strips of two-inch battening, in just the same way as described for the table-top (the one board can serve the two purposes). Now cut, also from one-inch board, a few thin wedges, each four or five inches long at least.

The method of using this clamp is as follows : place the work on the board in such a way that one end of it rests against one of the cross-pieces on the board. The space between the other end of the work and the other cross-piece is filled with wedges, which are knocked tight, and the whole job is then left for twelve hours or so until the glue is firmly set.

Something may here be said about making glue. Glue is bought by the pound at any oilmonger's or woodwork shop. The cake should be broken into small pieces and placed in the inner receptacle of the glue-pot (or in the jar or tin if no proper pot is used) and just covered with water. Leave the whole to soak overnight, or at any rate for four or five hours, then pour off the surplus water—that which has not been affected by the dissolving glue.

If you have a glue-pot you will not need instructions as to boiling, but if using a jar place it in a saucepan large enough to contain plenty of water in addition to the jar, otherwise the water will " boil away " before the glue is properly heated.

Use the glue hot. Its thickness should be about that of new cream, and it should run freely from the brush. An old rhyme in the trade says :

> *When glue is thick it will not stick.*
> *When glue is cold it will not hold.*

In glueing a joint smear the two parts with glue and quickly clamp them together before the glue begins to get cold. Then leave the work at least twelve hours in the clamp for the glue to set.

SIMPLE FURNITURE MAKING

WOODS TO USE

For the purpose of assisting the amateur unfamiliar with woodyards and the buying of timber, as many as possible of the jobs described on the pages that follow have been worked out to such dimensions that the timber required is " stock-size " and can be bought ready squared and planed up. Such stuff as 2″ by 2″ quartering, 5″ by 1″ floorboard, 2″ by ⅞″ battening can be bought machine-finished at little more than the cost in the rough, and the extra pence save a great deal of trouble, particularly for the amateur with only a few tools and no proper bench.

Such wood can be bought at any timber yard or woodshop, and it is cheap ; but it must be remembered that it is mostly deal or pine—" soft " wood that is unsuited for many jobs. As it happens, it *can* be used for all the jobs given in this book.

Nowadays, however, in every town there are shops which cater specially for the home carpenter, and supply nicely finished legs for chairs and tables and other pieces of furniture. These are in oak, mahogany and other harder woods and come a little dearer than similar work in common deal or pine, but they are much stronger, and they are capable of taking a splendid finish. Oak is particularly popular.

A word may be added with regard to ply-wood, which plays such a prominent part in modern furniture making. As is generally known, ply-wood consists of very thin slices of wood glued together in such a way that in each alternate layer the grain runs at right-angles to the grain in neighbouring pieces. The most common ply-wood met with is "three-ply," with two slices having grain running, let us assume, from north to south, and an intermediate slice with grain running from east to west. Ply-wood is very strong for its thickness, but it has certain peculiarities which the novice would be wise to respect.

In the first place, it is difficult to cut unless you go about it the right way. Probably the simplest method of cutting a piece of ply-wood is with a sharp knife. Pencil a cutting line on each side of the sheet and make deep cuts on each side—at least through the outer layers and into the centre layer. When these cuts have been made, turn the sheet so that they lie parallel to and just above the edge of the table. Lean on each piece of the sheet, and it will snap cleanly along the cuts.

Do not attempt to cut ply-wood with a coarse hand saw; the teeth will almost certainly tear the edges of the wood. Use a tenon saw, keep its edge more or less parallel to the surface of the wood, and bend the wood slightly so that its upper surface is convex. This convexity will ease the path of the saw as it travels to and fro in its cut; otherwise the saw is very liable to stick and the job becomes awkward.

Another point about ply-wood is its tendency to warp and bend. Odd pieces of ply-wood should be kept in a dry place and should be so stored that they are flat ; a temporary curve due to something leaning against ply-wood is liable to become semi-permanent and not easy to straighten out. Be very careful not to let ply-wood get wet, and if it does get wet do not hold it before the fire. The wet not only causes the wood to swell, but it softens the glue if it gets to it ; heating raises steam, and it is by no means improbable that a series of corrugations will ruin the surface of the ply-wood.

In nailing ply-wood, use only the thinnest panel pins. Owing to the peculiar make-up of a sheet of ply-wood anything stouter than a thin pin that is inserted anywhere near the edge is almost bound to split some part of the wood. Towards the centre of a sheet there is less need for this precaution, though no one is likely to use a two-inch cut nail to attach ply-wood that is only a quarter of an inch thick.

SECTION II

VERY SIMPLE BOOKSHELVES

For many reasons the most popular place for a bookcase is the recess beside the fireplace, but it is not generally realised that one can fill the whole of that space with strong bookshelves without driving a single nail or screw into the wall. Tenants of flats should try this method of fitting up their fireside recess.

Measure the width of the recess and cut your shelf to exactly an eighth of an inch less than that measurement. Before actually cutting the shelf, however, make sure, by measurement, that the two side walls of the recess are parallel; they are not always, and in such cases the ends of the shelves must be cut to the angle made by the walls. The shelf may be made from " fancy " woods, but with a little staining ordinary floorboard (5" × 1") can be made to look quite well. If the first shelf is made very carefully, it can be used as a pattern for the others, and all that will be necessary will be to lay it on the board and run a pencil along the ends where cut, but remember to allow for the thickness of the pencil when you come to cut the second shelf. Run the plane along the ends of shelves before fitting into position.

Now take the first shelf and place it across the

recess so that the ends rest on the skirting board, about nine inches from the floor (See Fig. 2). On this lowest shelf you will probably place your largest books. Stand a couple of these on the shelf and decide at what height you will want the next shelf above. Probably ten inches will be about the height. Now cut two pieces of floorboard, each ten inches in length, smooth the ends, and stand them at either end of the bottom shelf, and on their upper

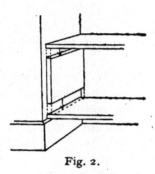

Fig. 2.

ends rest the second shelf. If the ends have been cut square, this second shelf will be found perfectly steady, and its steadiness will be increased when the shelf bears a row of books.

The rest of the shelves are made simply by repeating the above process. The shelves, in fact, are built up by means of end-slabs of desired height, each resting on the shelf beneath.

You may not desire shelves all the way up from the skirting, in which case the series may be begun at the chair-rail; but the handy man will quickly find ways to adapt this principle, which is very valuable to those forbidden to drive nails or screws into their walls.

The front edge of the shelves may be covered with leatherette fringing (which has the advantage that it hangs down and so keeps much dust from the books on the shelf below) or wooden moulding may be applied with glue or with very thin nails sold for the purpose. If moulding is fixed along the front edge of each shelf, and also on the end-slabs, and the whole dark-stained, it should look very well.

One advantage of such bookshelves is that they can be made with no other tools than a saw. Even the planing of the ends can be done by careful work with a sharp penknife. Most other bookshelves require the use of a chisel, since the ends of the shelves are fitted into channels cut in the end panels. There is something very pleasing about the construction of a well-fitting bookcase of such a design, but the beginner will find that there are several points to be carefully watched if that pleasure is to be his. Such a job can be done entirely with floorboard. The following is the method :

Having decided upon the width of shelf, cut off a sufficient number of boards to a length just half an inch more than the desired length of shelf. This will allow for the sinking of a quarter-inch of shelf into each of the end boards. In cutting the ends of the shelves, use a fairly fine-toothed saw, preferably a tenon saw ; a coarse-toothed saw will tear the wood and spoil a good fit. Similarly, when smoothing up

B

the cuts after the shelves have been sawn off, be careful to keep the end edges as sharp and free from "roundness" as possible. Needless to say, the saw-cut should be at right-angles to the surface of the shelf.

Now for the end boards. The length of these will depend upon your intentions concerning the "heads and tails," *i.e.*, the pieces above the top shelf and below the bottom shelf. In estimating the distances *between* shelves, do not forget to allow for the thickness of the shelf itself, or you may find that the space is too short to take the books intended for it.

For marking out the end boards you will require a square of some sort, in order that the grooves shall be precisely at right-angles to the edges of the end boards. Mark the boards with the exact thickness of the shelves, but in cutting them cut inside the line rather than outside. A tight fit can easily be remedied, not so a loose fit. In sawing the edges of the grooves keep the saw upright and level. You will have marked on either edge the depth to which the groove must reach—a quarter of an inch—and be careful not to saw beyond that mark ; it is better if anything to saw a little short of it at first.

If your groove is to be half an inch wide, it is best made with the aid of a chisel of that width, and since you will have a fair amount of such work to do in making a bookcase of this pattern, you may consider it worth while to buy such a chisel specially The outlay of a shilling or so will be justified by the cleanness and ease of the work.

VERY SIMPLE BOOKSHELVES

In chiselling out grooves start chiselling *from* the edge, towards the centre of the groove. When working the other way—outwards—there is a likelihood of the side of the board splitting away. Take the wood off in easy sections ; gentle taps with mallet or the side of a hammer, or even with the palm of your hand, are all that should be required.

Having cut and fitted your shelves, you will want to " bind " the structure to make it rigid. Glueing the ends of the shelves into the joints will do much towards this, but it is worth while to supplement it. Nails or screws can be driven through the end boards, but these are apt to be unsightly, though they can be punched home and the holes stopped and hidden by stain, etc. Nails can also be driven skew-wise into end boards from shelves so as to be invisible. A neat and simple way of binding the structure is to cover the whole of the back of the shelved portion with ply-wood, nailing and glueing it to the back edges of the shelves and the end pieces. The edges of the ply-wood can be concealed if the end pieces of the shelf are lined with a small wooden beading.

If the bookcase is to be of the hanging variety, and is to be heavily loaded, it is a good plan to attach two strips of batten to the back as shown in sketch (See Fig. 3). This is usually supplied 2″ by ¾″, and accordingly spaces must be cut in the backs of the shelves so that the battens will lie in them snugly and not project beyond the back of the shelves. The battens should be at the ends of the shelves, and nails or thin screws driven through them into the shelves and skew-wise into the end boards. A hole through the top of each batten will serve to hang the shelf with.

If this is considered unsightly cut a piece of ply-wood to fit above the topmost shelf and between the end boards so as to be in front of and conceal the projecting upper ends of the battens. If the tops of the end boards are covered with moulding,

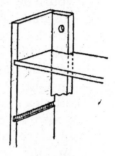

Fig. 3.

this should be carried right round the top of the ply-wood.

The appearance of the bookshelves will be greatly improved if they are fitted with glass fronts, which have the further advantage that they protect the books from dust. The front may be made in one piece, to cover the whole of the shelves, or each shelf may have its own cover, as in sectional book-cases. If this arrangement is adopted, the frames must be made to fit *between* the shelves. If they are hinged to the front of the shelves it will be impossible to open any section without first half-opening the section above, since the bottom of one frame will almost rest upon the top of that immediately below.

Frames may be made of 2" by ⅜" battening, the corners being joined by a simple mortise and tenon. Hints on marking and cutting mortises and tenons will be found on the pages relating to table making ; here it will be sufficient to include a diagram (See Fig. 4) showing how such a corner is cut and fitted.

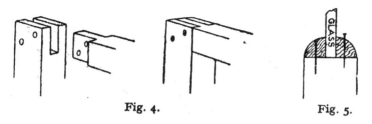

Fig. 4.   Fig. 5.

The glass is fitted to such a frame by means of two strips of thin quarter-round moulding (See Fig. 5), glued and pinned to the inner edges of the frame, one strip on either side of the glass, as shown in the diagram.

SECTION III

DESIGNING FURNITURE

BOOKSHELVES present few difficulties of design, but before proceeding to discuss the manner of making up tables, chairs and similar pieces of furniture a few observations may be made concerning the structure of furniture.

If the sides of three chairs are examined—an adjustable chair, a railed small chair, and a railless small chair—certain important differences will

Fig. 6.

become apparent. Each chair has four upright members, forming legs, and these legs are joined one to the other by horizontal rails. In the adjustable chair the rails are three in number (See Fig. 6, Diagram A). Each end of each rail is jointed to the leg, and when the six joints are made fast the five pieces of wood form an exceedingly rigid framework. This may be taken as typical of the strongest structure in general use. It is found in many kinds of furniture. Sometimes one or other of the rectangles, or even both, is filled with panelling which further strengthens the structure. In a dinner wagon, for instance, the lower rectangle is panelled ; in a filing cabinet both are panelled.

Diagram B (Fig. 6) may be taken as typical of a structure not quite so strong as A, but stronger, other things being equal, than C, which represents the ordinary small chair. In B, the legs and rails form a single closed rectangle, and if the joints are well made of hard wood the structure is very strong. It appears in such articles as small occasional tables, stools, umbrella stands, etc., and in many pieces of furniture having legs too slender to withstand the strain imposed when, as in C, only one rail is used to join each pair of legs.

It will be seen that in such a case (C) the corners where the rails and legs meet are subject to very severe strains, and for this reason such chairs should always be made of hard wood, and the joints should be very carefully cut and fitted, and good hot glue used to cement them. In type B the rectangle is often filled with panelling, which strengthens the structure, and the position of the lower rail may be high or low, according to requirements.

Taking these three types, any novice of average ability can· make up furniture that will be strong and presentable. Two forms of joint will suffice to unite the rails and legs ; one will be found fully described in the notes on joining table rails to the legs (in Section IV) ; the other can be practised in the course of making a simple stool.

SIMPLE FURNITURE MAKING

A Bathroom Stool

The stool will be a form of type B—*i.e.*, in addition to the top rails supporting the seat there will be strengthening rails between the legs lower down.

With the exception of the lower rails, which should be of quarter-inch stuff, all the wood can be cut from ordinary one-inch floorboard. The legs may be planed so as to taper slightly from top to bottom, or they may be left with parallel sides, though a stool with untapered legs is apt to look rather " stodgy." If each leg is 17″ long and a quarter of an inch narrower at the bottom than at the top that will be sufficient taper. In planing the taper, by the way, take wood from all four faces of the leg in equal quantities.

If your seat is to be thirteen inches across, cut the lower rails twelve inches in length. They should be about a quarter of an inch thick and rather more than an inch deep. Now at an equal distance from the lower end of the front pair of legs mark out a hole—known as a mortise—just large enough, but only just, to receive one end of the rail. The mortises should be in the centre of the leg-face and particular care must be taken to make them at equal heights from the ground, otherwise the rail will not lie horizontally. The mortise must now be chiselled out to a depth of five-sixteenths of an inch. Use a quarter-inch chisel, and make the hole smaller than intended rather than larger. The sides must go straight · down and be quite smooth and clear of splinters, etc. Fit the two ends of the rail into the mortise holes. If the fit is too tight, shave away a little of the rail with a chisel ; do not force the joint with a hammer, lest the leg splits.

Fig. 7.

Now take the other pair of legs and repeat the process, making the mortise holes in the same position as the first pair. This being done, you will have two H-like structures, which must be united by mortising rails similar to those already put in. These rails, however, should be inserted an inch or two lower than the front and back rails, for the sake of simplicity.

The seat slab is cut from two one-inch boards, about six inches in width, and glued edge to edge to form a solid slab about 12" wide by 13" long. Two ledges may be screwed and glued to the underside, across the grain, to hold the top boards firmly together. The top being made, it is placed over the legs so that the outer faces of each leg are flush with one of the edges of the top ; long thin nails are driven downwards through the top into the legs to hold them in this position.

With such a stool as this, it is not necessary to joint the top rails. It will be found that the stool is already fairly rigid, but to make it quite firm **four**

Fig. 8.

pieces of quarter-inch stuff about three inches deep must be fitted round the top, as shown in the diagram (See Fig. 8). These should project about a quarter of an inch above the top slab to form a receptacle for the cork seat—to be bought for sixpence or so at any cheap ironmongery or " chain " store. Each strip should be glued and nailed to the edge of the top slab and also to the tops of the legs. The glue should be given twelve hours to set, and then the stool can be sandpapered and enamelled. The lower rails may be secured additionally by thin $\frac{3}{4}''$ nails driven from the inner sides of leg.

UNEVEN LEGS

Should the legs be found to be of unequal lengths, so that the stool does not stand steadily, they can be adjusted in the following manner : Support the stool in such a way that it stands upright (on three legs). Now take an odd piece of the quarter-inch wood and lay it on the floor so that its edge rests against one of the legs of the stool. With a pencil mark round the leg the point at which the edge of the piece of wood comes. Do this to each of the legs and then saw off where marked. The stool will now stand steadily.

SECTION IV

TABLE MAKING

THE construction of such a stool as that just described is a very useful preliminary exercise for anyone about to make a table. The principal difference, apart from dimensions, concerns the fitting of the legs to the side rails. A further point which should not· be overlooked is that whereas the stool is of type B (See Fig. 6) and is fitted with strengthening rails, the table is of type C, in which all the strain is concentrated on the corners where the rails are joined to the legs. This fact should be borne in mind when making the joints, which should be of the best possible fit.

The form of joint described below is applicable to almost any kind of table, and we shall, therefore, deal with its construction in some detail, the more so since to the novice it is something of a mystery. One may look at the corners of a well-made table for hours without discovering how the parts are fitted together.

Since the novice will probably at the first attempt decide to make a kitchen table rather than one for the drawing-room, we give below a list of the materials required for such a table. The wood suggested is yellow deal, and the sizes mentioned are " standard," obtainable at any wood yard or wood-craft shop.

KITCHEN TABLE

Wood Required

2 lengths,	2' 11" long,	of	5" × 1" boarding.
2 ,,	1' 11" ,,	,,	5" × 1" ,,
2 ,,	1' 9" ,,	,,	5" × 1" ,,
4 ,,	2' 5" ,,	,,	2" × 2" ,,
3 ,,	3' 5" ,,	,,	9" × 1" ,,

After obtaining the wood, the first step is the marking of the legs, which are made from the four lengths of 2" quartering. These can be given a better appearance if slightly tapered, so that at the feet they are, say, half an inch thinner than at the top. This effect can easily be contrived with a plane, and the ten minutes' extra work is justified by the resulting improvement in the appearance of the table. Before beginning to plane, however, mark on each leg the amount of wood you desire to plane away; otherwise the result may be anything but symmetrical.

Now proceed to mark on the legs the positions of the mortise holes into which the side rails will presently fit. In each leg a slot, or mortise, must be cut five inches down to receive an end of a side rail, and a similar slot is required to receive the end of an end rail (See Fig. 9). These mortises are each 1½" deep, but they are so arranged that a certain portion of the wood cut away from the leg is common to the two mortises. It is important to bear this in mind when marking out the mortises so that they fall on the proper faces of the legs.

Taking the first leg, measure five inches down from the top and mark a line across two adjacent faces. Now, at a distance of one inch from one edge mark a line parallel to that edge and just five inches long, and half an inch farther in—*i.e.*, at one and a half inches from the edge—mark another parallel line. It may save possible confusion if the space between these two lines is roughly shaded with pencil; it represents the wood to be cut away.

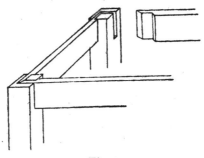

Fig. 9.

Proceed to mark out the other mortise. Be very careful that you select the proper face of the leg, however. A glance at the diagram should make the matter clear, but the rule is to work from the same edge of the leg for both markings. First mark a line at an inch from the edge and then a second line at one and a half inches from the edge. Once again shade in the space, $\frac{1}{2}''$ by $5''$, between these two lines ; it denotes wood to be cut away.

Now continue these lines across the end of the leg,

to ensure that the mortises shall be square to the faces of the leg, and once again shade the portion to be cut away. It will now be seen that the two mortises will join, and will isolate one small piece of the leg from the main part of the leg top. This small piece will be on the *inside* when we come to fit the table together—a little point worth remembering.

Having marked the mortises, and gone over the marking with a rule to ensure that it is quite correct, one may now begin the cutting out. The work may be started with a tenon saw, but most of it must be done with a half-inch chisel. Before beginning to chisel away any of the wood take the chisel round the edge of each mortise and with a light tap break the surface of the wood with the chisel edge ; this helps to prevent the wood from working " ragged " round the edge of the mortise while chiselling is in progress. In chiselling out, be content to take small pieces of wood at a time ; by taking larger pieces you are liable to split away more wood than intended and the joint will be weakened thereby. Care, too, must be taken to make the sides of the mortise straight and at right-angles to the face of the leg—another reason for taking away only small pieces of wood at a time. Those unused to chiselling out will certainly find it helpful if the sides of the mortise are sawn out as far as possible.

When chiselling out the second mortise in each leg, be careful not to split away any wanted wood when reaching the point where the two mortises overlap ; care and patience are required at this stage if the table is to be rigid and strong.

As each pair of mortises is chiselled out they should be smoothed and cleared of all " whiskers " and splinters : remember that these surfaces have to be glued to the rails so as to hold the table rigid, and the smoother the surfaces are the more strongly will they be held together by the glue.

The mortises finished, one may turn to the side rails. It will be noticed that although the mortises are half an inch wide, the rails are twice that thickness. The reason for this difference is to provide a " shoulder " on the side rail which forms a very important feature of the joint and upon which much of the rigidity of the table depends. To form this shoulder, take one of the side rails and at a distance of $1\frac{1}{2}''$ from the end mark a line at right-angles to the edge. This line should run across one face of the rail and over the sides. Now, from the end to this line, mark on each side a line just half an inch from each edge, and continue this line over the end of the rail in such a way that, when a saw-cut is made along this line and another saw-cut along the line on the face of the rail, a piece of wood 5" long by $1\frac{1}{2}''$ broad by $\frac{1}{2}''$ thick is detached from the rail. This leaves at the end of the rail a tongue or tenon $1\frac{1}{2}''$ long and $\frac{1}{4}''$ thick, which should fit snugly into the mortise in the leg ; but for this fit to be a good one it is necessary to mark and to cut most carefully, and it is better, among other things, to cut away too little wood, when making the tongue, than to cut away too much. Any surplus wood can soon be chiselled away until the joint is good. When the rail is in position it will be seen how the " shoulder " rests against the innermost corner of the leg and how valuable it is, when all is glued together, as an aid to rigidity.

Now proceed to treat each end of each rail in similar manner. Be careful to make tongues on the same side of each rail : a little inattention may easily put one wrong on this point, and it is a good plan to do here what was suggested when marking out the mortises, and shade with pencil those pieces of wood which are to be cut away.

We have purposely omitted one further treatment of the tongues that is necessary before any glueing can be done. It will be found, in short, on attempting to fit the table together that only two of the rails will fit properly into the mortises, the other pair being prevented from " going home " by the intrusion of the pair that does fit. The simplest manner of dealing with this is to mitre the ends of the four pairs of tongues—*i.e.*, take a triangular cutting from the tip of each tongue so that, when the fitted rails are looked at from above as they lie in the mortises, they converge in the same way as the corners of picture frames.

A much better plan, however, and one which greatly helps the rigidity of the table, is to cut, half an inch deep from the tip of each tongue, a simple joint that, adequately glued, will effectively interlock the two rails (See **Fig. 10**).

TABLE MAKING

Here it may be added that where the table is designed to stand considerable strains and where large legs are being used—as, for instance, a table to support a heavy billiard board—it is often advisable to cut one mortise right across the leg, with tongued rail to correspond, the other rail being locked into the first rail by a square tenon fitting into a mortise in the longer tongue (See Fig. 11).

If mortises and tenons are cut accurately as described and the joints are treated with good hot

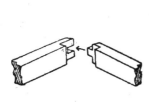

Fig. 10.

Fig. 11.

glue and left to set for about twelve hours, the table should be strong enough to stand ordinary usage without further support. Since, however, we are using this table as a demonstration of table making in general, it may be added that the rails may be locked to the legs by means of dowel pins—pencil-shaped pieces of wood fitted into specially bored holes. Dowel pins are superior to nails for such a purpose. For one thing, should it be necessary for any purpose to detach a rail or a leg, the wooden dowel pin can easily be removed with a bit or even

c

a gimlet ; removing nails would be a very different proposition. If nails are used they should be long and thin, and should be driven from the inside of the leg through the tenons into the outer portion of the top of the leg.

Having fitted, glued and clamped the lower part of the table, one may turn to the preparation of the top. This is formed of the three pieces of 3' 5" length, held together by the two 1' 9" pieces. An advantage of buying wood of this kind ready planed is that the edges will be square and that little adjustment will be necessary to get the three boards to lie closely together. The novice who sets out to plane the edges so that the boards fit closely will find it less easy than he probably anticipated.

The two 1' 9" ledges should be placed at right-angles to the top boards, of course, and should be about two feet apart. Be sure before screwing the ledges to the top that you have them correctly centred, otherwise the table top will project farther one side than the other when placed upon the stand. Glue the edges of the top boards and clamp them tightly together, the boards lying face downwards in the clamp. When the clamps have been wedged fast, the ledges may be fastened across the top boards, glue being used as well as 1½" screws—four screws for each board in each ledge.

Ample time should be allowed for the glue to set fast, and then the top may be fixed to the stand. The simplest way of fixing is by glueing the top edges of the rails and the tops of the legs and driving long thin nails downwards through the top into the rails, the nails being punched well below the surface of the top and the holes filled with stopping. A neater job may be made by turning the whole table upside down and driving long thin nails through the rails and into the underside of the top boards.

The top should now be given a good rubbing down with sandpaper, and the edges and corners rounded off with a plane.

Such a table as that described is easy to make provided due care is taken in cutting the tenons and mortises, and it will stand a considerable amount of hard wear.

Ornamental Tables

The foregoing method is applicable to almost every kind of table, with certain modifications that will be obvious when one comes to the job. Very light tables with spindly legs, for instance, need a strengthening rail near the lower ends of the legs, since there is very little wood to give strength where the rails meet the legs. Such rails are fitted to the legs by an ordinary tenon and mortise : a simple and quite effective way of making the mortise is to bore a round hole with a centre-bit, shaping the tenon accordingly. An even simpler way of strengthening the legs of an ornamental table is to add a tray, or " lower deck," attaching it at the corners to the legs by screws driven into the under-side of the tray and passing through the eyes of screw-eyes screwed into the inner sides of the legs (See Fig. 12).

Small tables not likely to be subjected to wet (such as the scrubbings given to a kitchen table) may be topped with ply-wood. This obviates the trouble of joining two or three boards neatly, and provides a perfectly smooth surface, free from the slightest cracks. A ply-wood top, however, needs rather stronger mounting than an ordinary board top. It is well, for instance, to glue to the underside of the four edges strips of wood at least $\frac{1}{4}''$ thick and as wide as the overlap. The ledges, too, might be three in number instead of two, and they should be let into the top edges of the rails so that the ply-wood top lies level with the rest of the rails. Small square pieces of wood may be glued in the angles between rail and top to make the fit even more secure.

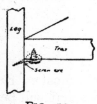

FIG. 12.

With a ply-wood top it is necessary to add a beading to the edge, since the edge of the ply-wood is rather unsightly. Beading is very cheap, and a few pennyworth of beading neatly pinned round the edge may make a remarkable difference in the appearance of the job.

SECTION V

AN ADJUSTABLE CHAIR

PURPOSELY we have described somewhat minutely
the making of a table, since when one has mastered
the knack of getting a really good fit between legs
and rails one can apply the facility to various other

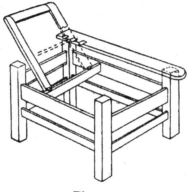

Fig. 13.

pieces of furniture which depend for their stability
on a similar joint. An obvious example is a chair.
If you have made a satisfactory job of a table, you
will find the construction of an adjustable chair easy
and rather more interesting than the table. This
type of chair is the best for the novice to tackle,
since all the joints and cuttings are straightforward,

while the design is such that any slight weakness in a joint that fits rather poorly does not seriously impair the utility of the chair (See Diagram A, Fig. 6). The chair has the further advantage for the amateur, moreover, that it is fitted with loose cushions, so that none of the intricacies of upholstery are involved.

It is not proposed to go into minute details of construction, since the chair is such that the amateur can easily prepare his own working design and make the chair large or small, high or low, to suit his own taste. It may be added that such a chair looks very effective when the legs are made simply from yellow deal, although it naturally looks more " finished " if specially turned legs are bought.

The front rail of the seat of such a chair is rather lower than that of an ordinary chair, averaging only twelve to fifteen inches from the floor. In estimating for the depth of seat, room must be left for the lower part of the adjustable back. The sides of the chair will require to be about a foot longer than the depth of the seat.

In making up, one cuts the four legs and joins them with rails as for a table, except that the rails do not come at the top of the legs, but about midway. The exact position depends upon the thickness of the cushioned seat and, of course, one's personal taste. These rails should be of 1″ wood and not less than 2″ or 2½″ deep. Below these main rails a lighter set is fitted into the legs, as in bathroom stool (See Fig. 7). If the main rails have been well fitted, these lower rails need not be so elaborately interlocked, and by placing those at the side just a little higher than those at front and back one can simply make good deep circular mortise holes with a brace and bit, and fit the rails with round tenons.

The arm rests should be cut $3\frac{1}{2}''$ or more in width and with plenty of overlap in front of the legs. They are attached by cutting a square mortise in the underside for each of the legs, to which they are attached by glue and a couple of long thin nails driven slantwise upwards through the leg into the underside of the arm. Be careful not to break the upper surface of the arm with these nails.

Before assembling the chair proper for glueing and dowelling, fix the supporting rail for the adjustable back. This should be tenoned into the two main side rails rather more than a foot from the back rail. It should be of the same width and thickness as the side rails, and the mortises in the latter should not, of course, be visible on their outer sides.

Now, too, should be cut in the arms the sockets for the supporting rod that will hold the adjustable back. The rod itself can be made most simply from a length of broom-handle, suitably sand-papered. At each end about an inch of the rod should be chiselled away until it is only half the circumference of the main portion of the rod : this will give the ends a diameter of about $\frac{3}{4}''$. Three pairs of semi-circular sockets should now be cut in the arms to receive these rod ends. The first pair should be about $2\frac{1}{2}''$ from the far ends of the arm rests ; the second pair $3''$ farther, and the third pair $3''$ from the latter : these distances, however, are quite arbitrary and may be varied to suit one's own ideas. The grooves should be about ½" deep and should be placed so that the rod rests at right-angles to the arms of the chair.

Assuming the lower part of the chair to have been made of 1" boarding, with legs 2" square, the adjustable back may be made of 2" × ¾" battening. Its general structure will be gathered from the diagram ; the back is fixed to the supporting rail by a couple of hinges.

So far, nothing has been said regarding a support for the seat, but we must now indicate the various ways in which this can be supplied. The simplest and least comfortable method is to screw a supporting ledge to the inner side of each of the main side rails and to place on these supports a series of 2" × ¾" battens. On these the cushions are placed.

A slightly better plan is to place a supporting rail on the inner side of each of the main rails and the front side of the rail which supports the adjustable back, and to screw to these rails short interwoven lengths of metal laths of the kind formerly used for bedsteads. The ends of the laths should be drilled to take the screws.

Perhaps the most satisfactory of the simpler methods of supporting the seat is to stretch upholsterer's webbing tightly across from rail to rail, interweaving it in the usual way. (For the manner of tacking and stretching this webbing, see *Simple Furniture Repairs*). When the webbing has been fastened in place it should be covered with a piece of material of a dark hue to match the cushions.

No special instructions should be needed concerning the making of cushions; they should be made too thick rather than too thin.

The finish of such a chair is a matter of personal taste, though probably some kind of oak or walnut stain will be chosen. Where the chair is for a bedroom or a room subject to much sunshine, such a chair can be very effectively enamelled white, and if the cushions are of a pretty bright chintz the final appearance will be very inviting.

SMALL CHAIRS

The ordinary small chair as used at table presents a fairly stiff problem for the novice, although his path has been to some extent smoothed by the fact that he can buy legs and backs ready for joining up. Excepting for the present Jacobean chairs, which have a secondary rail joining the legs only a few inches from the ground and thus giving them very valuable support and rigidity, the strength of the small chair depends upon the joints where the main rails join the legs and back; unless these joints are exceptionally well made and fitted, and the wood is hard, and the back legs are curved, the chair is not likely to be a success.

Another point which deters many novices is the difficulty of curving the back and legs gracefully.

They can, of course, be cut from the solid—and the task is less difficult than it might appear—but to cut a chair back and then to " finish " it satisfactorily are two different jobs, and it is not usually worth the trouble and the expense of the attempt unless one does it solely by way of amusement.

Novices who propose to make their own small chairs, therefore, are advised to go to a good wood-work shop and buy the legs ready prepared ; certain firms even sell complete chairs, ready for assembling, at a price which compares very favourably with what one would pay for the finished article at a furnishing house—one saves the cost of assembling the chair in a factory and also the greater cost of staining and finishing.

The novice who proposes to make a small chair will find all instructions for joints, etc., in the fore-going pages. The question of seating is dealt with more completely in the section on upholstering in *Simple Furniture Repairs*.

SECTION VI

CABINETS AND CHESTS

A Lady's Work Table or " Wireless " Cabinet

A USEFUL piece of furniture that is presentable in more than one sense of the word can be very easily made at a low cost by the novice with only a very modest tool chest. It is not proposed to give specific dimensions, since this is an article that anyone can design for himself, and the pleasure in making such furniture is infinitely greater than that found in carrying out the ideas of other people.

The job, however, introduces one or two practices which have not been described in the making of tables, chairs, or bookshelves, and since these practices are applicable in many ways it is proposed to deal with them somewhat fully.

Hitherto, for instance, we have used the rail merely as a support for the legs of chair or table. Here it fulfils another purpose, and instead of being somewhat concealed from view it becomes a prominent feature of the piece of work. In the work table illustrated (See Fig. 14) the rails are really panels. They are made of ply-wood, and are merely glued into relatively deep mortises cut in the legs. These panels have no " shoulders," like the rails of tables and chairs, but they make up for the loss of shoulders by their proportionately greater depth.   In fact, an 8″ ply-wood panel glued into a mortise makes a very strong holding.   In such a case as that illustrated the mortise would be in the centre of the leg, and about half an inch deep ; its width would be equal to the thickness of the ply-wood.

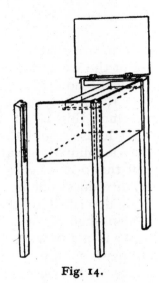

Fig. 14.

The bottom of the box, also of ply-wood, should be cut to fit round the legs and nailed (by means of panel pins) to the lower edges of the panels, and round the lower edges of these panels strips of suitable moulding are fixed

The lid should be large enough to overhang the legs ; it can be made of ply-wood, or of two ply-wood panels glued together ; but the effect will be much improved if it is made of thicker wood, say $\frac{1}{4}''$ oak, if the table is of that wood. A fillet about $1'' \times \frac{1}{4}''$ should be fixed to the top of the back panel inside to take the hinges. See that the hinges have leaves wide enough to lift the edge of the lid clear when it is raised : and in fixing the hinges it must be remembered that the legs project beyond the back panel to which the hinges are screwed.

Any ironmonger or woodworker's depot will supply suitable locks or handles, as well as a stay to hold the lid open when required. The little tray for pins, cotton, scissors, etc., is made to lift out. When in the table it is supported by two strips of wood glued to the front and back panels.

The finish will depend upon the kind of wood used and the maker's taste ; but moulding round the edge of the lid and at the bottom of the panels will do much to improve the appearance, as also will a small ornament in the front panel. These ornaments can be bought for a few pence at a woodwork stores, and are simply glued on to the panel.

A word of warning may be added with regard to the use of these panels as rails. Great care must be taken, in glueing the work together, that all four legs are parallel and that they will stand square to the floor. All should be well if each panel is slipped into its mortise to the full extent and so glued ; but an additional check may be made by measuring the diagonals of each aspect of the table and comparing results. Thus, if the distance from the top of the right-hand front leg to the bottom of the left-hand front leg equals that from the top of the left-hand front leg to the bottom of the right, then the front pair of legs are parallel to each other and the front section is a true rectangle ; but if one measurement is greater than the other it means that something is not quite straight, and steps should be taken to straighten it before glueing up. Such a point is of considerable importance in a tall slender article. The best way, of course, is to work step by step with a square, checking all angles as one proceeds.

The handy man will see at a glance that such a table can be adapted to form a very useful cabinet for a " wireless " instrument.

A Gramophone Stand and Record Cabinet

It is inadvisable to use such a design, however, when seeking to convert a table model gramophone into a pedestal model, since the weight of the instrument and records and the motion of winding the spring are liable to cause the joints to break away. Such a stand nevertheless is simply put together by adapting the " B " type of structure (See Fig. 6). The legs should be fairly stout—at least $1\frac{1}{4}$″ square—and both sets of rails should be securely jointed to the legs by means of mortise and tenon. The distance between the top and second rails should be at least 14″ to allow plenty of room for 12″ records to be stored on edge.

When the eight rails and four legs have been

securely fitted together panelling is inserted into the spaces between the side and back pairs of rails. (For method of fitting ply-wood panelling see that for fitting glass to bookshelf fronts in Section II). The space in front between the top and second rail should be filled with a hinged door. This can be made merely of ply-wood, to match the other panels, or a door can be framed up and panelled in the same manner as the bookshelf fronts. The amount of moulding, and its pattern, will be governed by the finish of the gramophone for which the stand is being made.

A Child's Cot

A job well within the scope of the amateur of average ability is the construction of a child's cot, especially as framed springs may be purchased at a reasonable price, together with the brackets for fixing them to the corner posts, and also nickelled fittings for drop sides. In cases where the springs are bought, the cot will be made to fit, so that it is not proposed to give dimensions here, but it may be mentioned that the corner posts are usually made about $1\frac{1}{2}''$ square. The side and end rails can be cut from $\frac{3}{4}''$ stuff and the panelling from $\frac{1}{4}''$ stuff.

The top and bottom rails of the back and the two ends are fitted into the corner posts by mortise and tenon joints of the kind described in the notes on chair and table making, but the lower rail in front is tenoned and fitted into mortises cut in the lower end rails instead of into the corner posts. This is done in order to leave room for the drop side. If there are iron-framed springs attached to the corner posts by special brackets this front rail may be dispensed with.

Before finally assembling these rails, it is necessary to cut mortises to take the splads which fill the spaces between the rails. This is the most tedious part of the job; and in case one is tempted to minimise the number of splads it must be remembered that they are intended to prevent the young occupant of the cot from getting or falling out; they also serve to give the structure increased rigidity. One way of lightening the task is to use round rods instead of flat splads, dropping the ends into holes of suitable size made in the rails with the aid of brace and bit. But it must be admitted that the flat splads look much better than the rods, especially when enamelled white.

As already remarked, one can buy special fittings for drop sides, but they are easily made (See Fig. 15). The drop side is cut and the splads fitted as for the back, the length of the top and bottom rails being such that they will just pass easily between the two corner posts. Two lengths of metal tubing, about $\frac{3}{8}"$ in diameter and 3" shorter than the corner posts will be required. Cut four triangular brackets from an odd piece of the 1" wood, each side being about $2\frac{1}{2}"$ long, and by means of dowel pins and glue fix one at the foot of each of the two front corner posts, in such a way that they will support the lengths of metal tubing in small holes drilled in their upper edges. Now, at a distance to correspond with the distance of the metal tubing from the corner posts, drill through the top and bottom rails of the drop side holes half an inch in diameter, through which the metal rods can pass. Thread the rods through these holes, place the lower ends of the rods in the triangular brackets, and over the upper ends place the remaining pair of brackets, fixing them to the

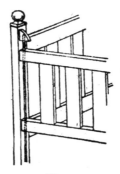

Fig. 15.

corner posts by dowel pins and glue. It may be found possible to get metal substitutes for these wooden brackets : they would be preferable.

The drop side is now free to slide up and down, guided by the metal rods. It only remains to fix a catch or bolt which will secure it in position. This bolt should be stiff in action ; else it will be slipped by unauthorised fingers and the occupant of the cot may get into trouble. The legs of the cot should be fitted with easy-running castors.

D

SIMPLE FURNITURE MAKING

Wooden Bed-Ends

One can buy bed springs framed in iron, and also the brackets by which they are attached to the bed-ends. All that remains, therefore, is the construction of the head and foot pieces of the bed—not at all a difficult task. The principle of design should be type B (See Fig. 6). That is to say, each pair of legs will be united by two strong horizontal rails,

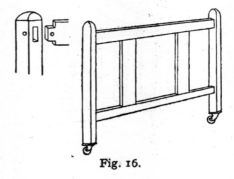

Fig. 16.

firmly tenoned and mortised and further secured by wooden dowel pins. The space between the two rails can be left clear if the bed is a narrow one, such as a child's bedstead, but it is usual to insert one or two splads, or even to fill the entire spaces with panelling. This is a good plan to adopt when making a child's bed, since on the panelling can be fixed coloured transfers, or with a fretsaw one could cut out the child's monogram or initials, or one or two fancy figures. The upright members should be made of 2″ quartering. For small single beds deal is strong enough ; but for wider beds it is desirable to employ a harder wood. The woodwork shops sell turned and moulded uprights and rails for bed-ends.

Space will not permit of detailed descriptions of all the various pieces of furniture which the average amateur can make ; on foregoing pages we have introduced him to a sufficient number of methods to enable him to put into practice most of his ideas. Nor need he feel afraid to tackle tasks that would a few years ago have been well beyond his scope : the mouldings and panellings and ornaments to be bought so cheaply at any woodworker's store to-day will help him to imitate the works of the professional furniture maker with considerable success. As an example of the manner in which the various methods given on foregoing pages may be combined we will indicate a simple way of making :

An Oaken Hall Chest

The chest is founded on four corner posts, 2″ square and about 18″ to 2′ high. Into these posts are tenoned and mortised four rails at the top and four an inch or two from the bottom, so that a short length of each corner post projects as a leg. Between the top and bottom rails in front and back two splads are let in, two or three inches in width and so spaced as to divide the front opening into three equal parts. Into these three openings, as also into the end openings and the back, ply-wood panels are fitted.

(For method of fitting see notes on fitting glass to bookshelf fronts, in Section II.)

The lid is best made of heavy oak, but expense may be saved by making it of ordinary deal boards glued and dowelled together at the edges and sandwiched between two pieces of oak ply or veneer, glued on. Around the edge of the lid a carefully selected moulding is attached with glue and panel pins, and it may be that one can find an old brass hinge or two. "Reproductions" can be bought,

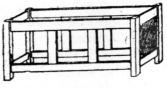

Fig. 17.

but they are naturally more expensive that those the ordinary ironmonger sells.

The whole chest may now be given a good rubbing down with sandpaper and stained and *judiciously* polished. Whatever you do, do not varnish it!

A SIDEBOARD

A sideboard may seem a very ambitious project for the amateur, but anyone who has made the oaken chest just described will not have the slightest difficulty in making a sideboard on the same lines. The principal difference in construction is that for a sideboard the corner posts are about 3′ 9″ in length, and that instead of the hinged lid access to the interior is given by a pair of doors in the front.

The corner posts are united by four pairs of rails, the upper edge of the topmost set lying (in the same way as table rails) flush with the tops of the posts. The top may be of deal, with a veneer of some finer wood over it. Ordinary birch ply, although cheap, looks well when stained. The backs and ends are panelled as in the case of the oak chest, but the lower

Fig. 18.

edges of the panels are held on the inner side by the bottom of the cupboard, formed of ordinary boards, the ends of which overlap by half an inch the lower rails, being supported by a ledge midway. Shelves inside the cupboard rest on ledges attached to the corner posts.

The cupboard doors call for careful measurement and cutting, but present no terrors to the pains-taking worker. The corners can be joined by an ordinary open mortise and tenon, the centre being filled with panelling in the same way as the sides and back of the sideboard. The doors should be made to lie as closely as possible together when shut, and a small lock or catch fitted. The angles of all the panelling may be filled with moulding or left plain. If the woodwork is carefully done and the whole finished in, say, walnut, the effect is certainly pleasing without any moulding, as it is in oak ; but a simple moulding in these angles takes away a certain austerity that is noticeable if all the angles are clean right-angles. Any appearance of bareness about the four corner posts can be remedied by the application of a small ornament such as a very small fruit and flower cluster (hardly bigger than a half-crown) glued on about six inches from the top.

SECTION VII

STAINING AND POLISHING

THE secret of success in " finishing off " a piece of work is to have a perfectly smooth surface on which to lay the stain or polish. Planing is not enough. Fold a piece of fine glasspaper over a block of wood or cork, about 4″ by 2″, and rub and rub until the surface seems incapable of improvement, and feels like silk. Then take some plaster of Paris and mix it to a thin cream with some of the stain it is proposed to use, and rub this cream well into the pores of the wood. When the plaster has had time to set, and not before, scrape the surface of the wood with the edge of a piece of glass or steel until all is smooth again, and then finish off with sandpaper. The wood is now ready for the stain.

Not long ago, amateurs wishing to stain furniture had either to buy a varnish-stain mixture guaranteed to dry with a gloss that was not to everybody's liking, or had to go in search of such weird ingredients as " dragon's blood "—rather like some of the Borgias' potions. But now all kinds of stains and finishing sets can be bought for a few shillings, and it may be said at once that many of them do what they claim to do—make it possible for the amateur to imitate very closely the work of the professional polisher. A little practice is desirable before attacking the real job, and such a trial is after all only fair to the makers. Since full instructions are included in the sets, and these instructions vary according to the materials used, it is not necessary to outline the processes here. Instead we will give a few hints for those using the simple water stains and other less elaborate processes.

Any oilmonger or woodwork shop will supply for a few pence sufficient powder to make half a pint or more of good stain by the simple addition of warm water. These powders are named according to their results when applied in solution to woodwork, " oak," " walnut," " mahogany," and so on. They can be bought direct from the chemist under other names at a saving of perhaps a penny, but the novice who wants to be certain of getting the right tint with the least trouble should get a proper powder. The application of such a stain is extremely simple. One can use a brush or a pad, for the solution is so thin that there is no chance of brush-marks, and it is almost difficult to apply the stain unevenly. One or more coats may be given, according to the density desired.

There are now three alternatives. The stain may be left as it is, unprotected by size or varnish ; it may be given a coat of varnish ; or it may be rubbed up with beeswax or furniture polish. For oak and walnut, the last-mentioned course is much the best, resulting as it does in a fine gloss yet that is not the unnatural shininess that often goes with varnish. The polish or wax should be applied fairly liberally, and rubbed in : elbow-grease is even more necessary than beeswax. No other directions are necessary. From time to time the wood should be given a fresh application of wax and rubbing, and it will quickly attain an excellent surface.

Those who prefer to varnish over their stain may be recommended first to give the stain one or perhaps two coats of strong size, to " set " the stain. Size is bought at an oilmonger's and melted from jelly to liquid, like glue ; it is then applied with a brush. Novices may be warned that it has an evil smell when warm. About a quarter of a pound of size to a quart of water is a good proportion.

There is a great deal of mystery about the processes of french polishing, but the secret of success, as in all such work, is careful preparation and plenty of patience. There are various recipes for making up french polish, and almost every oilmonger has his own polish, as well as the several proprietary brands he also sells. The simplest for the amateur to make is compounded of orange shellac and spirits of wine in the proportion of one ounce to one pint.

French polishes are applied with a pad, the method of using which should be clearly understood. Each pad consists of a central ball of cotton wool or flannel, over which is stretched a covering of old linen—a piece of old handkerchief is just the thing. The inner ball is intended not only as a cushion but as a reservoir for the polish, and by judicious squeezing of it polish is fed as needed to the rubbing surface of the pad. A large amount of rubbing and a small quantity of the polish are required, and after the first few strokes, during which the polish is spread over the surface, all work should be along the grain of the wood.

Varnish stains bought ready mixed are much used for odd jobs, and their application presents few difficulties. The novice may be warned against coating the wood too thickly, and also against going over the surface a second time before the first coat has had time to harden. All strokes should be made in the same direction, and an old brush should be used in preference to a new one on account of its freedom from loose hairs and the greater softness brought about by use.

A simple method of attaining very good effects is to coat the work with " flat " light stone paint—a deep cream colour. Give the paint ample time to harden, and then go over the whole with a coat of Brunswick black thinned out with turps. Simple as the procedure is, surprisingly rich effects can be attained with a little care.

SECTION VIII

KITCHEN ACCESSORIES

AN IRONING BOARD

ONE or two articles of kitchen furniture may be easily made by the novice. The first is a sleeve board for ironing. The sketch tells practically all that is needful. The board is made from 1" stuff, the top

Fig. 19.

piece being anything up to 2' long and tapering from 5" to about 3" and then running off to a point. The base board is about 15" long. The end piece is 5" square and the centre piece 5" × 3½". The back piece should be marked and cut as shown in the diagram, and dovetails made on the ends of the top and bottom pieces to fit snugly into this end piece. The simplest way of ensuring that the angles of the dovetail correspond to the mortises in the end piece is to place the latter against the end of the uncut top and bottom pieces in turn and to mark on them the exact shape of the mortise. When sawing and chiselling out, be careful to allow for the thickness of the pencil used to mark out with.

The centre piece is let into quarter-inch-deep grooves cut at right-angles across the top and bottom pieces. The whole may be held together with four two-inch nails. The top piece should be padded before use.

A Clothes Horse

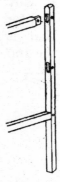

No instructions should be needed for this. The diagram indicates the method of mortising and tenoning the rails to the posts, and they should be either glued or dowelled in position. The sections of the horse are hinged together with bands of upholsterer's webbing; do not use metal hinges, or they will mark any damp clothes with which they come in contact.

Fig. 20.

A Clothes Airer

Two end pieces are cut from 1″ board, each 2′ 6″ × 6″. They can be left rectangular (See Fig. 21), but a little work with plane and saw or a stout penknife, or, better, a spokeshave, will suffice to turn out the ends to the shape indicated and add to the appearance of the finished job. Now prepare five rails, each of 2″ × 3″ battening and of a length to suit the room, and six inches from each end of each rail cut a notch one inch wide by one inch deep. In each of the two end pieces cut five similar notches

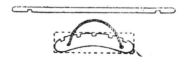

Fig. 21.

$1'' \times 1''$ (make sure that these notches are directly opposite to each other). Do not nail the rails to the end pieces, for fear of marking any clothes; the joints should be cut closely enough to hold without nails. Holes should be bored in the end pieces, when all is ready, to take the cord.

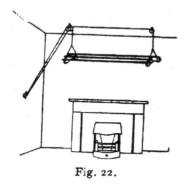

Fig. 22.

The rail is suspended from the ceiling by one double pulley and one single pulley. These pulleys must be screwed into the joists, and to find these, examine the floor of the room above. Measure the distance between any selected row of nails and the wall, and apply these measurements to the ceiling below ; the right joist will soon be located. A cleat will be necessary to secure the cord when the airer is pulled up.

These airers have two distinct advantages over the old-fashioned clothes horse. They are pulled up near the ceiling out of the way ; and they considerably lessen the risk from fire.

HOUSEHOLD STEPS

It is easier to make a pair of steps than many novices imagine. All that is necessary is careful work ; no great skill is needed.

For the side pieces ordinary 5″ × 1″ floorboard will do very well. Select boards that are free from large knots likely to weaken the whole. Lay them side by side and knock two nails through so that the boards are temporarily held close together : this will facilitate marking out and ensure that the steps shall be even. The marking is all-important. First, from each end of the pair of boards measure 4½″, and draw two lines at right-angles to the edges of the boards. Now draw two diagonal lines (See A in Fig. 23) and saw the triangular pieces left from each end of the pair of boards. This will ensure that each side will stand firmly on the floor and will lean forward to the same extent. Your steps should be about

9″ apart, so now mark off along one edge of the boards a series of points each exactly 9″ from the other ; turn the boards over and do the same along the other edge (See Fig. 23).

The boards may now be separated, and each should be clearly marked with an " in " and an " out " side. On the " in " sides draw lines between the

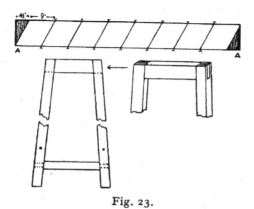

Fig. 23.

V's on the edges, and one inch below each line draw another. Each of these pairs of lines represents the groove to be cut to receive the end of a step. Having cut the grooves and cleared them of splinters, etc., the actual steps may be cut, also from 5″ × 1″ floorboard. It will be noticed that the lower steps are wider than those near the top : this tapering helps the stability of the steps. The lowest step may be about 16″ ; the top about 9″. If these two are cut

59

and fitted (due care being taken to get the steps and sides four-square) the remaining steps can be cut to fit merely by measuring the distance between the bottoms of the respective grooves. Steps should be nailed in position.

Immediately below the lowest step but one a piece of 5″ × 1″ should be let in, its upper edge being nailed to the back of the step and its ends nailed to the side pieces ; and another piece of 5″ × 1″ should be nailed across the back of the steps at the top. Finally, the top piece should be put on, overlapping each side by about three-quarters of an inch.

The strut may be formed by ripping a piece of the 5″ × 1″ board into two pieces, 2½″ wide by 4′ 10″ long. Plane them up and then mortise and tenon, almost at right-angles, a piece of 5″ × 1″ at the top, and, 18″ from the bottom, a piece of 2½″ × 1″. The legs of this strut should be splayed to the same extent as the uprights of the steps. The joints should be well made and secured with glue and a single screw each. The strut is fixed to the steps with a hinge, and two lengths of sash-cord are passed through holes lower down to adjust the strut to the right distance of extension. When this has been decided, shave the lower ends of the struts so that they lie flat on the floor.